THIS BOOK DONATED BY:

Jeremy
Konstanzer
1-2-95

ANIMAL MIXUPS

by Millicent Selsam and Joyce Hunt
illustrated by John Wallner

Macmillan Publishing Company   *New York*

Maxwell Macmillan Canada   *Toronto*
Maxwell Macmillan International   *New York   Oxford   Singapore   Sydney*

Macmillan Publishing Company is part of the Maxwell Communication Group of Companies.

Macmillan Publishing Company, 866 Third Avenue, New York, NY 10022

Maxwell Macmillan Canada, Inc., 1200 Eglinton Avenue East, Suite 200, Don Mills, Ontario M3C 3N1

First edition. Printed in Hong Kong.

1   3   5   7   9   10   8   6   4   2

The text of this book is set in 22 pt. ITC Century Light. The illustrations are rendered in watercolor.

Library of Congress Cataloging-in-Publication Data
Selsam, Millicent Ellis.
Animal mixups / by Millicent Selsam and Joyce Hunt ; illustrated by John Wallner. — 1st ed.
p.   cm.   Summary: Simple text discusses how different kinds of animals live in different places
and reproduce their own kind. ISBN 0-02-778081-3   1. Animals—Miscellanea—
Juvenile literature. [1. Animals.]
I. Hunt, Joyce.   II. Wallner, John C., ill.   III. Title.
QL49.S36 1992   591—dc20   91-16114

For
Stephanie
Howze
—M.S. & J.H.

For
Ray, the Bear,
Jimi,
and Billy Ray
—J. W.

Some things belong together.

Some do not.

Do these babies belong to these mothers?

No, they do not.
Turn the page to see who belongs to whom.

Do these animals belong in the desert?

No. The desert is too hot and dry
for walruses and polar bears.

Camels and deserts go together.

But walruses and polar bears live where there is snow and ice and water.

Are there giraffes or zebras where
there is snow and ice?

No. Giraffes and zebras live on the plains where there are some trees, lots of grass, and it is warm.

Here are three animals.
Two of them live in the forest. One does not.
Which one is it?

The whale belongs in the sea.

Here are some other animals in the sea.
Find the one that does not belong there.

Monkeys live in the trees and swing from branch to branch.

What's going on here?
These legs are all mixed up.

Now the legs are on the right animals.

Tails can get mixed up, too.

Now the tails are not mixed up.

What's wrong with these pictures?

Rhinos have horns.

Elephants have trunks.

These skeletons are next to the wrong bodies.
Match each one with its owner.

Now, turn the page to see where the skeletons belong.

Do cows lay eggs?

Do chickens give milk?

No. Chickens lay eggs.

And cows give milk.

Are these animals in the right place?

They are not.

Birds build nests.

Spiders spin webs.

Something is wrong with these
pictures, too.

Can you see what it is?

Do rabbits eat spaghetti?
Do children eat grass?

No. Rabbits eat grass.

And children eat spaghetti.

Some things belong together.

Some do not.